Unleash your creativity and embark on a delightful adventure with "Monkeys Unbound," a charming coloring book that brings to life the enchanting world of monkeys.

Immerse yourself in the captivating realm of these spirited creatures as you color your way through 15 mesmerizing illustrations.

Each page features a unique monkey design, intricately detailed to spark your imagination and provide hours of relaxation and entertainment. "Monkeys Unbound" offers a collection of captivating illustrations that cater to colorists of all ages and skill levels.

Allow your inner artist to flourish as you explore the boundless possibilities of color and shading. "Monkeys Unbound" is not only an invitation to unwind but also an opportunity to unleash your artistic potential. So, grab your favorite coloring tools, and let your imagination run wild in this enchanting adventure.

Discover the joys of "Monkeys Unbound" and join these lively creatures on an unforgettable coloring experience.

This Creative Adventure Belongs To:

____

Embrace your boundless creativity and embark on a
delightful voyage with these creative monkeys

EverEndlessDesigns is an artistic endeavor rooted in the idea that creativity knows no bounds. It represents an unyielding passion for exploring the endless potential of imagination and bringing to life unique and captivating illustrations.

At the heart of EverEndlessDesigns lies a commitment to nurturing and celebrating the limitless possibilities of artistic expression. Through a diverse range of enchanting and whimsical designs, it seeks to inspire and empower individuals to delve into their creative depths and discover their own unique artistic voice.

"Foxes Unbound" embodies the spirit of boundless creativity that drives EverEndlessDesigns. This collection of stunning illustrations is designed to provide colorists of all ages with a captivating and immersive experience that encourages exploration, self-expression, and the joy of artistic discovery.

As you embarked on your way in this adorable journey through the fun of "Foxes Unbound," may you find inspiration in the enchanting world of EverEndlessDesigns and unlock the infinite potential of your own creativity.

Here's to the boundless adventure of artistic expression, and to the wondrous journey that lies ahead.

Checkout our more products at everendlessdesigns.store

Monkeys Unbound: EverEndlessDesigns Coloring Collection

Conceptualized and Created by: Andy Broyles
ISBN: 9798390416754